REAL WORLD ECONOMICS

Why
Banks
Fail

Amy Sterling
Casil

+6.73

+1.23

+21.64
+14.83
+3.24
+32.47
+2.35
+9.19

+11.02

+25.06

ROSEN
PUBLISHING

New York

22.95
12-10

To my students at Saddleback College, Mission Viejo, CA

Published in 2011 by The Rosen Publishing Group, Inc.
29 East 21st Street, New York, NY 10010

Library of Congress Cataloging-in-Publication Data

Casil, Amy Sterling.
Why banks fail / Amy Sterling Casil.
    p. cm.—(Real world economics)
Includes bibliographical references and index.
ISBN 978-1-4358-9462-4 (library binding)
1. Bank failures—United States—Juvenile literature. 2. Banks and banking—United States—Juvenile literature. I. Title.
HG2491.C374 2011
332.10973—dc22

                                                                2009041635

Manufactured in the United States of America

CPSIA Compliance Information: Batch #S10YA: For further information, contact Rosen Publishing, New York, New York, at 1-800-237-9932.

On the cover: Stock exchanges around the world, including the London Stock Exchange, experienced turmoil on September 15, 2008, with the failure of U.S. investment firm Lehman Brothers.

Contents

INTRODUCTION

The Great Depression is the name of the international economic crisis that occurred from 1929 to 1934. It was a time of bank failures and a loss of trust in the banking system. During those years, more than ten thousand banks failed.

In December 1929, the Bank of the United States became the first major bank failure during the depression. Despite the bank's name, there was no connection between the Bank of the United States and the federal government. The Bank of the United States was founded in New York in 1913 by Joseph S. Marcus, a garment manufacturer from New York's Lower East Side neighborhood. Marcus's bank specialized in lending money to recent immigrants. The bank's name was meant to inspire the immigrants' confidence in the bank's safety. The Bank of the United States operated less conservatively than many other banks at the time. It made risky loans to customers who could barely afford to pay back the loans.

In October 1929, the U.S. stock market crashed, causing many investors to lose all of their money. Customers began to withdraw large amounts of money from the Bank of the United States, either to make up for losses in the stock market or to pay for their basic needs. By December, the bank had lost $40 million, or about 30 percent of its reserve funds. On December 8, a previously announced merger with three other New York banks was called off.

News of the bank's struggles reached the public, and on December 10, 1929, more than 2,500 customers withdrew a combined amount of $2 million from one of the bank's branches in New York. The scene attracted a crowd of over twenty thousand. The crowds and the public panic represent a classic run on a bank. The term "bank run" refers to a large number of customers seeking to withdraw money from a bank at the same time.

The *New York Times* reported that the run on the Bank of the United States was caused by a false rumor, but customers

In 2006, U.S. investment firm Bear Stearns was fined $250 million by the New York Stock Exchange for risky investments, including mortgages, in an event predating the economic recession of 2007.

continued to form long lines at all of the bank's branches, asking to withdraw their money. The next day, the New York State superintendent of banks closed the Bank of the United States.

The Bank of the United States had four hundred thousand depositors—more than any other in the country. At the time, the failure of the Bank of the United States was the largest in U.S. history, and it remains a symbol of the Great Depression. At the end of the depression in 1934, thousands of banks had failed. The U.S. government created new bank regulatory agencies and passed laws in order to prevent the financial suffering of millions of families from happening again. However, there is no guarantee against bank failures.

CHAPTER ONE

What Is a Bank Failure?

A bank failure is the closing of a bank by a federal or state bank regulatory agency. Regulatory agencies close banks after they fail to meet their obligations. A bank's obligations are to pay money that is owed to depositors, investors, and creditors. Banks earn money by lending money to customers. Customers then pay the amount that was lent to them back over time, usually in monthly payments that include additional money, which is called interest.

What Happens When a Bank Fails?

Banks are responsible for meeting the demands of the customers who have deposited money in the bank. A bank officially fails when it cannot give every customer the money he or she has deposited on request. A bank becomes unable to cover all of its deposits when its debts, or the money it owes, are significantly larger than its assets. The assets of a bank include cash,

A run on a bank can involve hundreds or thousands of customers. These customers are lining up after the failure of IndyMac Bank in Southern California on July 14, 2008.

investments, and the value of loans that the bank has made to customers. A bank's debts include deposits and payments due on bank investments. Banks also loan money to other banks and receive interest payments from other banks.

In July 2008, Pasadena, California–based IndyMac Bank failed. IndyMac Bank was founded in 1997 by Countrywide Financial, a southern California–based company that specialized in nontraditional mortgages. IndyMac's main business focus was to lend money for many different types of mortgages on homes and land. Both Countrywide Financial and IndyMac expanded rapidly during the housing boom that occurred in the United States between 1996 and 2006.

The housing boom was a period when home prices increased rapidly. The estimated value of a home is also referred to as equity. The price and equity increases encouraged many homeowners to obtain money for home improvements, vacations, college tuition, and other needs by taking out additional mortgages based on the estimated value of their homes, called home equity loans.

Between January and June 2008, several smaller banks had failed in different parts of the United States. The largest bank failure prior to IndyMac Bank was ANB Financial, which had

IndyMac

Business experts began to notice IndyMac Bank's financial losses almost immediately after home prices and home sales slowed in California. Negative stories about the bank's earnings began to appear on television and the Internet. In June 2008, U.S. senator Charles Schumer, who served on a Senate committee regarding banking, wrote a letter to the Federal Deposit Insurance Corporation (FDIC), the government organization that regulates banks in the United States, asking that the agency take steps to prevent IndyMac's failure.

The letters written by Senator Schumer set off a panic among customers, and many made a run on the bank. Worried customers withdrew more than $1.3 billion from IndyMac in eleven days. On July 12, 2008, the FDIC stepped in and closed the bank.

After taking over, FDIC officials quickly told customers that they could continue to use ATMs, debit cards, and checks.

Normal branch hours, online banking, and phone banking services resumed Monday with the bank operating under the new name IndyMac Federal Bank. All customer deposits at IndyMac Bank of up to $100,000 were insured by the FDIC. Most IndyMac customers did not lose all of their money; unfortunately, most IndyMac Bank investors and stockholders did.

$2.1 billion in assets at the time of its failure. The majority of the other banks that failed in the summer of 2008 had assets of less than $12 million, which is very small for a financial institution.

Government oversight plays an important role in bank regulation. U.S. senator Charles Schumer conducts a press conference following a meeting with Assistant Treasury Secretary Neel Kashkari on October 15, 2008.

In contrast, IndyMac Bank was a large bank, with more than $32 billion in assets. Many of the mortgage loans that IndyMac Bank made relied on steadily increasing property values to justify the amount of money that was loaned. If property values decreased, the value of the bank's mortgages on the homes and land would decrease. By spring 2008, IndyMac Bank had already lost money, with many risky mortgages beginning to fail. A failed mortgage is one where the customer can no longer afford to make the monthly mortgage payment. The worst type of failed mortgage is one where the customer is no longer able to make payments, and the home or land is also difficult to sell.

Companies, including banks, can sell stock to investors to obtain money, which is also called capital. A bank's stock reflects the value of its profits and its long-term earning power. At its highest point in 2006, IndyMac Bank's stock was trading for more than $50 a share. After the bank's failure in July 2008, the same stock was trading for ten cents a share. In order to understand the volume of loss to stock investors, imagine if a person bought a $5,000 bicycle and then one year later found that he or she could only sell it for $20.

How Many Bank Failures?

A total of more than ten thousand banks failed in the United States during the Great Depression. Most of the banks that failed during this period of time were small. Bank failures rose and fell between the 1930s and 1980s. The 1980s were the period of time when bank failures began to rise again. Many financial crises in the 1980s were related to financial institutions that are similar to banks, called savings and loans.

The primary purpose of savings and loans are to help customers save money to purchase homes and land. The types of products and services they offer are limited. Deposits in savings and loans were insured by the Federal Savings and Loan Insurance Corporation (FSLIC) between 1934 and 1989. In 1989, the FSLIC was overwhelmed by repaying the deposits of many customers of failed savings and loans that went out of business during the ten-year savings and loan crisis. The FSLIC's responsibility was passed to the FDIC, which currently insures deposits at participating savings and loans in addition to bank deposits.

One cause of the 1980s savings and loan crisis was a real estate boom in both commercial and residential projects that occurred during the 1970s. Many savings and loans lent money for real estate projects during this time. As the boom continued, the loans that were made became riskier. Then the U.S. economy slowed down in the late 1970s and early 1980s. Stagflation occurred, which is a serious economic problem. The word "stagflation" combines economic "stagnation" with "inflation," which is a rapid rise in the price of goods and services.

Economic conditions in 1981 were very difficult. The U.S. gross domestic product, or GDP, declined 2 percent. Mortgage rates reached 21 percent, and the prime rate for banks to lend money was 21.5 percent, the highest rate ever achieved. Inflation was 14 percent, which means that the prices for products that people wanted to buy increased much faster than they could earn money. On average, between one hundred and two hundred banks failed each year in the United States throughout the 1980s. During the worst year of the crisis, 1989, more than five hundred banks failed. Overall, during the savings and loan crisis (1986–1995), 2,377 banks failed, representing 67 percent of

The Great Depression lasted for more than ten years. Here, the unemployed wait for food outside a Salvation Army soup kitchen in 1935.

U.S. bank failures between 1934 and 2008. At the worst time of the crisis, one savings and loan or bank failed every 1.38 days.

Between 2004 and 2007, the United States experienced the longest period in its history with no bank failures—nearly three and a half years. According to the official list maintained by the FDIC, no banks closed or failed in the United States between June 25, 2004, and February 2, 2007.

Since the beginning of the worldwide recession that developed in 2008, more than ninety banks have failed in the United States, and hundreds of other banks have failed worldwide. However, not all countries experienced high rates of bank failures at this time. Banks and investors worldwide began to study banking practices in Canada, which had not had a single bank fail during the world crisis. In 2008, the World Economic Forum ranked Canada's banking system number one worldwide. In contrast, the United States placed fortieth in the rankings, behind many other countries with varying types of banking systems. In August 2009, *Global Finance*

magazine evaluated and selected the world's fifty safest banks. The safest banks included German, Dutch, Swiss, Canadian, and Australian financial institutions. The highest-ranked U.S. bank was the Bank of New York Mellon at number twenty—a 225-year-old bank that specializes in investment banking and asset management.

In 2008, U.S. financial regulatory agencies extended $6.8 trillion in temporary loans, liability guarantees, and asset guarantees in support of banks. By April 1, 2009, the total amount of the new U.S. government financial programs to assist banks exceeded $13 trillion. How much is $13 trillion? One-trillion dollars equals $1,000,000,000,000, or twelve zeroes to the left of the decimal point. It would take a military jet flying at the speed of sound, reeling out a roll of dollar bills behind it, fourteen years before it reeled out one trillion dollars.

CHAPTER TWO
Why Do Banks Fail?

Bank failures have been a problem throughout the history of banking. Bank failures were recorded in ancient Egypt and Greece. In ancient Greece, a sacred building on the Acropolis, a hill that housed temples and other important buildings, was burned in order to conceal a bank fraud scheme. Historical records show real estate fraud that caused other ancient Greek and Egyptian banks to fail. Modern financial experts and countries across the world are struggling to understand the problem in today's banking system and what can be done to solve it.

As the U.S. economy grew in the nineteenth and early twentieth centuries, the banking industry grew even more rapidly. Many small banks were established all across the United States. Economic analysts, according to John R. Walter, believe that the rapid growth in the numbers of banks overbuilt the industry. In the early 1920s bank failures increased, leading up to the economic crisis of the Great

Bank failures have been recorded throughout history. The Acropolis, in Athens, Greece, was the site of an ancient fire that covered up a bank failure.

Depression. At the height of the depression, two thousand to three thousand banks failed each year. The high numbers of bank failures ended in 1934, when the U.S. government passed laws to form the agency that currently oversees bank

operations and insures bank deposits—the FDIC.

U.S. Federal Reserve Board chairman Ben Bernanke says that the events of the Great Depression "and its lessons are still relevant today." Headlines written during the Great Depression match today's headlines. According to Bernanke, these headlines featured "high unemployment, failing banks, volatile financial markets, and even deflation."

How Subprime Mortgages Led to Bank Failures

In the 1990s a new mortgage industry began in the United States. This was the subprime mortgage industry. A prime mortgage is a traditional mortgage, where the borrower must be able to prove that he or she has sufficient income to make the mortgage payment each month. Borrowers provide proof of income through their bank statements, pay stubs from a job, or tax returns. Traditionally, lenders would not issue a prime mortgage to any customer with monthly payments higher than 30 percent of their monthly income.

19

Many different forms of subprime mortgages began to emerge, including loans where customers merely had to state their income with no proof required. Other mortgages were issued for monthly payments of much more than 30 percent of

Orlando, Florida, residents protest the predatory lending practices of Countrywide mortgage lenders on October 9, 2007. Citizen protests can call attention to unfair bank lending.

the borrower's income. Financial experts came up with a special term for the most extreme subprime mortgages: a NINJA loan. NINJA is an acronym, or abbreviation, standing for "no income, no job, no assets."

In December 2008, *Business-Week* writers Chad Terhune and Robert Berner traveled to Miami, Florida, to investigate the mortgage crisis and NINJA loans. They interviewed eight residents at Palmetto Towers, two eight-story condominium buildings acquired by a subprime lender in 1996. All eight residents interviewed at Palmetto Towers said that they had agreed to mortgage terms that required them to make mortgage and condominium fee payments that were much higher than the government guideline of 31 percent of their monthly income, a requirement for loans received from the Federal Housing Administration (FHA).

Four of the eight owners said that they received cash payments of $10,000 or more when they completed, or closed, their mortgages. The cash payments were offered to them in order to encourage them to buy the condos. The payments are not legal, and the extra money was included in the overall total of their loans. A resident named Sascha Pierson was a full-time student receiving a $42,000 annual education grant meant to pay for her housing and education. She received an incentive of $19,500, which was called a cash-back opportunity. Her educational grant was scheduled to run out, and Pierson did not know how she would pay her mortgage in the future.

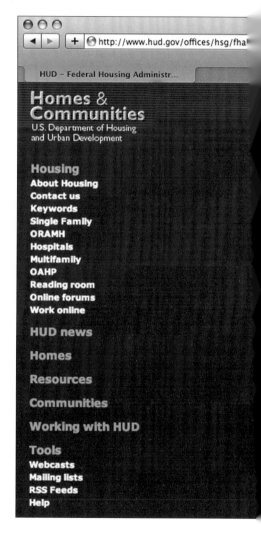

Pierson's neighbor, twenty-seven-year-old Lorena Merlo, received an incentive of $14,640 in April 2008 when she purchased her three-bedroom condominium. Merlo, a part-time legal assistant, and her husband, Renny Rivas, a drywall laborer, earned a total of $52,000 a year and had two young sons. Their monthly home payments amounted to 58 percent of their income, way over the FHA, or commonsense, limit of a manageable mortgage payment. "We are four months behind on our mortgage," Merlo said.

The loans that the residents of Palmetto Towers received were part of an FHA homebuyer program. The FHA, which is a government agency, provides mortgage insurance. The money required for the mortgage insurance program is added to each buyer's monthly mortgage bill. Similar to the FDIC deposit

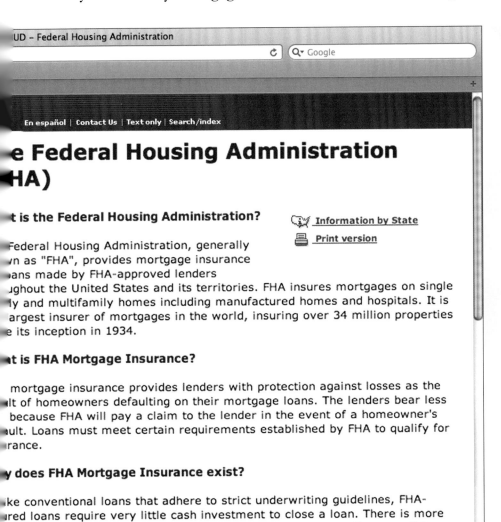

UD – Federal Housing Administration

En español | Contact Us | Text only | Search/index

e Federal Housing Administration HA)

t is the Federal Housing Administration?

Information by State

Print version

Federal Housing Administration, generally
vn as "FHA", provides mortgage insurance
ans made by FHA-approved lenders
ighout the United States and its territories. FHA insures mortgages on single
ly and multifamily homes including manufactured homes and hospitals. It is
argest insurer of mortgages in the world, insuring over 34 million properties
e its inception in 1934.

t is FHA Mortgage Insurance?

mortgage insurance provides lenders with protection against losses as the
lt of homeowners defaulting on their mortgage loans. The lenders bear less
because FHA will pay a claim to the lender in the event of a homeowner's
ult. Loans must meet certain requirements established by FHA to qualify for
rance.

y does FHA Mortgage Insurance exist?

ke conventional loans that adhere to strict underwriting guidelines, FHA-
red loans require very little cash investment to close a loan. There is more

The Federal Housing Administration (FHA) was one of the agencies created by Congress to provide home ownership opportunities and expand mortgage lending.

insurance program that will refund up to $250,000 of funds that customers have deposited in a failed bank, the FHA mortgage insurance will pay off the mortgage in case the borrower is unable to repay.

According to the FHA, the agency insures mortgages on single family and multifamily homes, including manufactured homes and hospitals. It is the largest insurer of mortgages in the world, insuring more than thirty-four million properties since it began in 1934. The FDIC, which insures bank deposits, also began in 1934. Both government agencies were created in response to the Great Depression.

The FHA was not designed to provide insurance for residents making mortgage payments much higher than they can afford, like the residents of Palmetto Towers. In December 2008, 66 of the 158 condominiums in Palmetto Towers were in foreclosure. Foreclosure is a legal process that occurs when a borrower is unable to pay his or her mortgage payments for an extended period of time. The lender, a company called Great Country Mortgage, provided 1,855 FHA mortgages since November 2006. As of October 31, 2008, 923 of Great Country's loans were in default proceedings, which meant that the borrowers were unable to pay their mortgages. Great Country's 50 percent default rate was the highest in the entire FHA program. The borrowers' inability to pay the mortgages from Great Country Mortgage represents on a small-scale the larger worldwide mortgage crisis that led to bank failures in 2008 and 2009.

Many mortgages in the United States and across the world lost their value as more and more people became unable to meet their monthly mortgage payments. Banks were forced

Bank Failure in a Small Town

A notable failure during this time was the Oakwood Deposit Bank in Ohio, which was closed in 2002. A small bank, the Oakwood Deposit Bank had been in business for ninety-five years when suspicious checkwriting activities alerted the Federal Bureau of Investigation (FBI) to potential fraud. When FBI investigators closed in, they discovered that the Oakwood Bank's CEO, Mark Steven Miller, had taken over $42 million of the small bank's deposits for his own use. Miller, who also held several other titles at the small-town bank, including vice president and chief financial officer, was arrested, convicted of embezzling the funds, and sentenced to fourteen years in prison.

"Embezzlement" is a legal term that refers to an owner or an employee of a company stealing money secretly, using fraudulent business techniques. Miller's motive for taking the money from the Oakwood Bank was that he wanted to invest the money in gambling boats in Florida and South Carolina. The owners of the gambling boats were also conducting illegal financial activities. They were also arrested, tried, and convicted for their role in the scandal.

Since 1905, the Oakwood Bank had been a trusted part of the community, serving all seven hundred residents of the small town of Oakwood, Ohio. At the time of its failure, the Oakwood Bank had $102 million in deposits. Of the deposits, $9 million were uninsured (referring to accounts containing more than the $100,000 then insured by the FDIC). Organizations that lost money due to Miller's fraud included the village of Oakwood, the local school district, the local hospital, and a church.

to foreclose on many different types of properties. However, banks often found that they were unable to sell the properties to other buyers. Even when banks could sell the properties, they were often sold for much less than the original mortgage loan.

As a result, many trillions of dollars were lost by nearly every bank, large and small, across the United States and globally.

Three Main Causes of Bank Failure

In general, there are three main causes of bank failure: 1) lost customer confidence resulting in a run on the bank; 2) a credit crunch that reduces the amount of money the bank can borrow, often as a result of poor lending decisions made in the past or of larger economic crises; and 3) fraud or theft by bank officers or employees.

First, customers can lose confidence in a bank, often after hearing bad news about the bank's business. A real-world bank isn't like a piggy bank, where all the money is kept inside it. Banks only keep a portion of depositor's money on hand at any one time because they know that under normal circumstances only a small percentage of customers will ask to withdraw their money on a certain day. They lend the rest of the money out, often to

A Seattle branch of Washington Mutual is shown on September 26, 2008, the morning after it was seized by FDIC regulators and sold to JPMorgan Chase.

other banks, and receive interest, or earnings, on the money they lend.

A bank run occurs when many customers withdraw their money during a short period of time. Customers can lose confidence in a bank's ability to keep their money safe based on news reports of problems, statements by government officials, and through word of mouth. America's sixth-largest bank, Washington Mutual, failed in September 2008 after customers withdrew $16.7 billion in ten days.

According to Kathy Kristof, a financial reporter for the *Los Angeles Times*, IndyMac Bank, which once had ten thousand employees, fell prey to a "classic run on the bank." Federal regulators interviewed by Kristof said that warning letters written by Senator Charles Schumer to the FDIC and three other federal agencies were released to the public and helped bring about the massive withdrawals that caused the bank to fail.

Second, bank failures can be caused by a credit crunch.

"Credit" is a financial term that refers to the amount of money that a person or a business, including a bank, can borrow. Banks often borrow money from other banks to cover investments and other costs of doing business. Banks rely on

In September 2009, a locked and closed bank in Bridgeport, Connecticut, illustrates the high rate of poverty in the city, its struggling economy, and the prevalence of failed banks.

their credit rating, which is issued by business evaluators such as Standard & Poor's, to be able to borrow money that they need. Banks with a good rating from business evaluators can borrow money easily. However, if a bank has made too many bad or default loans, which are loans that are not paid back, the bank's credit rating can be lowered. If the bank's rating is lowered, then it can't borrow money easily. Sometimes, the bank's credit rating becomes so low that it is unable to borrow any money at all, which frequently leads to bank failure.

Other reasons for a credit crunch include a sudden increase in the rates charged for interest on loans, which is what occurred in the 1970s and continued into the 1980s. In 1965, if a customer wanted to buy a $40,000 house, he or she was asked for $6,000 as a down payment and received a mortgage for twenty-five years with a 5.5 percent interest rate. By 1970, the same buyer applying for a loan of $40,000 would make a down payment of $15,000 with a mortgage interest of 8.5 percent. In 1981, interest rates reached their highest level in one hundred years—more than 20 percent. At this time, few people wanted to borrow money for a mortgage or other type of loan, and as a result, bank earnings shrank dramatically. The high interest rates contributed to making the 1970s and early 1980s a time of high inflation, which is an economic term that refers to a steady increase in the cost of products and services.

Bank failures may also be caused by actual fraud. Bank administrators and employees can misuse funds and destroy the bank financially. Suspicious activity at a bank is usually reported to investigative agencies like the Federal Bureau of

Investigation (FBI) and to regulatory agencies like the FDIC. In 2002, the U.S. banking industry was concerned because after stabilizing the savings and loan crisis, they believed that bank failures were on the road to being eliminated. Then during the first three months of 2002, six banks failed, after only four banks had failed during all of 2001. Two of the six banks that failed during the first three months of 2002 were Internet banks whose business models were unstable. The other four banks that failed during the three-month period all failed due to fraud and mismanagement.

CHAPTER THREE

The Growth of Bank Failures

Many economists believe that bank failures are a fact of life because of an economic cycle called boom and bust. The primary way that banks make money is by lending money, then receiving the interest on those loans as the loans are paid back. Times of rapid economic expansion are referred to as boom periods. During these periods, some banks project very optimistic earnings from interest on loans. The banks take on a financial risk, which can become a financial loss if more than the average number of loans made during a boom period are not paid back.

The bust period occurs when the economic boom slows down. More and more borrowers become unable to pay back the loans they received during the boom period. The type of loans that are most vulnerable to boom and bust cycles are real estate loans. Small, medium, and even large banks that lent out too much money during economic boom periods are those at greatest risk of failure when the bust period arrives.

Japan experienced a serious economic bust in the 1990s, when many Japanese banks failed as a result of real estate loans

Mortgage lending that can lead to bank failures may be for residential homes or business property. Commercial real estate loans for large buildings contributed to the Japanese real estate and banking crisis of the 1990s.

made during a rapid real estate boom in the 1980s. Between 1985 and 1990, the six largest Japanese banks made $216 billion in real estate loans, primarily for commercial buildings and businesses. The bust period began in 1991, when the value of commercial real estate in Japan's largest cities, like Tokyo and Osaka, fell by 75 percent.

Trouble in Small and Medium-Sized Banks

The first effects of poorly performing loans are usually felt by small and medium-sized banks. A bank credit crunch, as opposed to an individual credit crunch, occurs when borrowers can no longer pay back significant loans to banks. As increasing numbers of loans given by small and medium-sized banks for construction projects during a housing boom period became delinquent, less and less capital was available for future loans or to cover interest owed by the banks themselves. In 2008, financial writer Alastair Barr of MarketWatch observed that the first group of poorly performing loans "hammered some small lenders that grew too fast during the recent real-estate boom."

News Reports Can Reduce Consumer Confidence

One important factor that contributes to bank failures is contagion. The U.S. Congress created the FDIC in 1934 to inspire customer confidence in the safety of banks. The FDIC's deposit insurance and regulation of banks was designed to prevent a recurrence of the contagion that led to the failure of one out of three banks during the 1930s. Economists and financial experts use the term "contagion" to refer to the process by which one bank's failure causes mistrust and fear in customers, leading other banks to fail. Contagion may also refer to the failure of one bank causing the failure of another bank that had loaned money to the failed or failing bank.

The training, administrative, and support divisions of the FDIC are housed in its satellite headquarters in Arlington, Virginia.

Today, financial news and rumors spread rapidly over the Internet. As an example, customers withdrew billions of dollars from IndyMac Bank and Washington Mutual in 2008, directly leading to the failure of both institutions. The customers heard about the low earnings and struggles of each bank through Internet business reports.

Scientists Research How People "Make a Run" on Banks

Researchers have suspected for years that like the flu, a bank run is contagious, spreading from person to person. In 2009, using computers and detailed bank records, finance professor Manju Puri at Duke University and Rajkamal Iyer from the University of Amsterdam teamed up to analyze a bank run that occurred in India in 2001. The researchers already knew that a nearby bank failure had encouraged a second bank failure in the Indian state of Gujarat. Minute-by-minute bank transactions during the three-day withdrawal frenzy at the bank were entered into a database. Then, assistants in India were given mobile GPS devices and transmitters and went to the addresses of the bank customers who had withdrawn their funds. The information was then mapped onto Google Earth. By comparing dates and times of withdrawals and the home addresses of customers, the scientists saw that the customers had decided to withdraw funds based on social and family ties. Customers who withdrew their money within the same period of time often lived in the same building. Analysis of the times of the withdrawals showed that the bank run was most contagious in its early stages and lessened over time.

How Mortgage Lending Can Increase Bank Failures

In September 2008, bank failures worldwide began with what financial experts call the mortgage crisis. A mortgage is a long-term loan made by a bank to individuals or businesses so they can purchase real estate by paying a portion of the loan back each month. Mortgages are a major source of income for banks because when customers pay back their mortgages, they also pay interest. Mortgages are given to customers to buy real estate, such as houses, condominiums, land, or business property. Under average circumstances, when the customer who has a mortgage becomes unable to pay back the mortgage, the bank goes through a process called foreclosure. Foreclosure allows the bank to sell the property—usually a home or land—which will reduce the financial loss on the property.

The 2008 mortgage crisis occurred for complicated reasons. One reason for the crisis was that many mortgages were made for a much higher value than the house or land was worth. This phenomenon was called the housing bubble. According to MSNBC senior financial news producer John W. Schoen, the housing bubble occurred because banking, real estate, and mortgage industries "believed that as long as incomes kept going up, people could afford ever-bigger mortgages and pricier homes." Another reason for the mortgage crisis was the increase in subprime mortgage lending. Subprime mortgages were non-traditional, risky mortgages that did not follow the same strict guidelines as prime or traditional mortgages.

On September 7, 2008, as a result of the loss of billions of dollars in nonperforming or toxic mortgage loans, the U.S. government seized control of the two largest mortgage

Four former CEOs of Freddie Mac and Fannie Mae testify before
the U.S. Congressional Committee on Oversight and Government
Reform on December 9, 2008.

corporations in America, Fannie Mae and Freddie Mac, com-
mitting up to $200 billion of taxpayer money to make up for
losses in failed mortgages. Fannie Mae was established as a
federal agency in 1938 in order to provide more mortgages

MR. BRENDSEL

for individual families and was chartered by Congress in 1968 as a private shareholder-owned company. Freddie Mac is a similar government-sponsored enterprise (GSE) chartered by Congress in 1970 "to stabilize the nation's residential mortgage markets and expand opportunities for home ownership and affordable rental housing." Both Fannie Mae and Freddie Mac had provided many mortgages to homeowners that were in default, and they were losing billions of dollars. The loans were not provided directly to customers. Banks provided the loans on behalf of Fannie Mae and Freddie Mac. Together, the two organizations were responsible for over half of the home loans in America.

In addition, the housing bubble had fueled an industry in mortgage-backed securities. Between 2000 and 2006, investment companies and lenders, including Freddie Mac, had created security funds made up of many different individual mortgages issued by multiple banks. In turn, other investment companies and banks purchased these securities. The original intent of the mortgage-backed securities was to spread the risk of financial loss if borrowers failed to pay back mortgages.

According to Freddie Mac, the giant lender uses "mortgage securitization to fund millions of home loans every year." Freddie Mac purchases home loans that lenders, usually banks, originate and then combines the loans in mortgage securities that are sold around the world. Profits from the sale of the securities are supposed to be provided back to the original banks and lenders. However, if people cannot pay back the mortgages that are part of the securities, there are no profits. Instead, financial losses spread and can lead to bank failure.

Cascading Bank Failures

Sometimes, one bank failure may lead to another. A series of bank failures is called a cascading bank failure. According to the financial magazine the *Economist*, the large number of small and medium-sized banks in the southern United States and their business practices contributed to a series of severe cascading bank failures in 2008 and 2009. Dan Blanton, the head of Georgia Bank and Trust, a community bank that did not fail, tells the *Economist* that "There were too many banks to begin with." Traditionally, in Georgia and other southern states,

Housing "boom" periods of rapid construction can lead to "bust" periods where little construction and lending occurs. A construction worker frames a house during a rapid building period.

most banks were established based on county charters, or rules that restricted them from branching outside of their area. Therefore, the southern states had many small, local banks instead of a few large ones.

Many of the small community banks in Georgia became financially overextended during the state's population and economic boom in the 1990s and into the 2000s. According to the U.S. Census, Georgia's population grew by 1.5 million people between 1999 and 2009. As a result, the new residents needed new housing quickly. Small banks could not afford to lend large amounts of money for new housing construction. To obtain the money to lend for construction, the small banks offered high-yield certificates of deposit to out of state customers. A high-yield certificate of deposit pays more than the average amount of interest. When the financial crisis of 2008 began, the out of state investors that had purchased the high-yield certificates quickly withdrew their deposits from the small banks in Georgia.

Georgia's small banks also banded together in "participations," a term for a multibank loan, which was pioneered by Silverton Bank in Georgia. Silverton Bank made more than five hundred group loans between 2000 and 2009. When Silverton Bank failed in May 2009, the small banks that were part of these group loans immediately lost money, causing a chain reaction, or cascading bank failure.

As of September 2009, more than ninety banks had failed in the United States during the economic crisis and recession. According to MarketWatch, in August 2009 economic experts predicted that as many as 150 U.S. banks and other lending institutions could fail before the recession ended. Some experts even predicted that more than one thousand banks would fail before economic recovery occurred.

MYTHS and FACTS

MYTH If a bank fails, depositors will lose all their money.

FACT Individual deposits are insured up to $250,000 by the FDIC.

MYTH It is safer to keep money in your house than in a bank.

FACT Banks are safe, as long as the financial checks and balances are in place.

MYTH Banks only fail due to incompetent or dishonest practices.

FACT Economic crises mean that even well-run banks can be at risk.

CHAPTER FOUR

The Effects

Bank failures, if they occur in large numbers, hurt more than the individual bank depositors, investors, and the employees who lose their jobs. Banks lend money to businesses and individuals to buy equipment, supplies, commercial property, and individual homes. The evolution of the financial crisis that began in 2008 began with rapidly dropping prices in the United States' residential home-buying market, which quickly spread to Europe, the United Kingdom, and Asia. The number of unsold homes increased as buyers waited for prices to continue to drop. Slowing prices reduced the potential for investments. Interest rates on home loans began to rise, reducing second-home purchases, and further decreasing the demand for homes. Many people chose to continue to rent rather than buy a home, even if they could afford a home purchase.

During the housing boom period, banks had provided adjustable mortgages, with interest rates and payments that increased two to three years after the initial home purchase.

During periods of widespread financial crisis, some communities are more devastated than others. A real estate sign on a foreclosed home in North Las Vegas, Nevada, in February 2009, shows a community devastated by the mortgage crisis and bank failures.

These mortgages began to reset in 2007, which meant that the initial low interest rates increased and so did monthly payments. Mortgage interest payment resets continued in 2008 and 2009. Previously, borrowers kept their payments lower by refinancing their homes before the adjustable rates increased. The new loans also featured low introductory interest rates. However, rising numbers of late payments on loans caused lenders to tighten standards, limiting the ability of subprime borrowers to refinance. In addition, falling home prices and slowing demand limited the owners' ability to sell their homes.

By January 2007, 14.3 percent of subprime loans were at least sixty days late, almost twice as many as were sixty days late in January 2006. A median category of loans, called Alt-A loans, had a much lower rate of late payments—only 2.6 percent. However, this rate had doubled from the 1.3 percent late payment rate in January 2006. Foreclosures continued to climb, and by March 31, 2008, 2 percent of single-family homes were in foreclosure and 6.4 percent of all mortgages were delinquent by thirty days or more. Of the mortgages that went into foreclosure in the first quarter of 2008, 50 percent were subprime mortgages, but another 42 percent were prime loans—in other words, loans where the borrower was evaluated as having an excellent chance of repayment.

Impact on Segments of the Economy

The mortgage crisis is not the only concern for consumers and financial markets. In June 2009, the *Los Angeles Times* reported that American credit card debt totaled $915 billion, a 435 percent increase since 2002. The amount of credit card debt is about the same size as the total of subprime or at-risk mortgage loans. Similar to mortgage-backed securities, about 45 percent of U.S. credit card loans have been packaged in groups that have been sold to banks and other investors. Credit card companies have already written off about 5 percent of unpaid credit card debts, which means they have decided the money will never be repaid.

Internationally, the effects of the 2008 banking crisis in the United States were felt far and wide. Before the crisis, U.S. banks were considered to be highly regulated, and, therefore,

America's banking industry made decisions that caused international problems, including financial instability in Eastern Europe and Russia. Russian President Dmitry Medvedev is shown in September 2009 at an international scientific conference.

investments with them were considered to be safe. The rise in severe financial losses from the mortgage crisis and subprime lending industry affected nearly every country in the world because banks and investment firms around the world had purchased the mortgage-backed securities. In October 2008, Russian president Dmitry Medvedev told a reporter for the *International Herald Tribune* that "the financial crisis signaled the end of U.S. global economic dominance." At the same time, Germany's finance minister, Peter Steinbrück, told an interviewer at the *Economist* that the United States was "the source … and the focus of the crisis" and was no longer the world financial superpower. The loss of confidence in the U.S. banking industry among international markets will probably take many years to resolve.

World confidence in the U.S. banking system is important because as of 2009, U.S. government debt reached a record $10 trillion. Individual U.S. consumer debt was even larger at $14.5 trillion, and unfortunately, U.S. savings rates remain low. Where did the borrowed money come from? Foreign investment provided support for the large sums of money owed by the U.S. government and individuals.

The Role of Credit in Business Investment

Bank failures can reduce credit and lending to the point where business development slows or even stops. One example of this negative effect is Japan's real estate and investment banking crisis. In the 1990s, a real estate and investment boom occurred in Japan. Financial experts called the rapid Japanese economic expansion a bubble, which soon burst. The bubble

A Bank "Marriage" and Its Effects

Washington Mutual's failure and instability in major investment firms and insurance investment companies led to the U.S. Congress passing an emergency act to improve the crisis in October 2008. Among many other provisions, the emergency act authorized the FDIC to insure deposits of up to $250,000. The increased amount of depositor insurance was put in place for a limited period of time, between October 2008 and December 2009.

A merger or marriage between a failing bank and a stronger bank will probably help the average depositors of the failing bank. People who had shares of stocks or bonds tied to the failing bank will not usually be so fortunate. The deposits of WaMu account holders were guaranteed by the FDIC up to $100,000 and additional deposits were guaranteed by JPMorgan Chase, which purchased WaMu's remaining assets for $1.9 billion.

Depositors' money was safe, but JPMorgan executives immediately planned to begin laying off WaMu employees and consolidating branches in areas where JPMorgan already had bank branches. As many as five thousand WaMu employees were at risk of losing their jobs.

By taking on all of WaMu's troubled mortgages and credit card loans, JPMorgan Chase absorbed at least $31 billion in losses that the FDIC would have otherwise had to pay to depositors from the insurance fund.

occurred primarily in commercial real estate and international investments. Banks grew too fast and made too many risky loans. When these loans began to fail, this caused instability in Japan's banking industry. Japan has a regulatory agency similar to the FDIC in the United States. In Japan, the agency is called the Deposit Insurance Corporation (DIC). The Japanese government and the DIC intervened in the banking failures, but they were slow to take action.

Japanese banks became less and less able to make any new loans after the banking crisis occurred. The effects of the burst bubble discouraged business investment by Japanese corporations. Japan's economy began to shrink. With the economy contracting, Japanese banks lost even more money. Japan's financial system and economy became trapped in a vicious cycle. Japan entered a period of recession.

Japan had only begun to recover from its economic recession when the United States' mortgage crisis occurred in 2008. Japan's recovery slowed and then stopped as its banks again lost their ability to extend large amounts of credit to businesses to expand and offer new products.

The Role of the FDIC in U.S. Banking Stability

Government regulations can help prevent bank failures, especially if problems are identified early and steps can be taken to correct them. The FDIC visits banks regularly to monitor their operations. FDIC bank examiners perform tests and review bank records to ensure that they are operating according to federal regulations. In addition, banks pay a premium, or specified amount of money, to the FDIC each year for an insurance

The FDIC is the federal agency responsible for monitoring bank performance and stability. FDIC chair Sheila Bair reports on the quarterly bank performance in November 2008 in Washington, D.C.

fund that will return depositors' money in the case of a bank failure. To be insured by the FDIC, a bank must prove to the FDIC that it is being run profitably and fairly.

Banks have always paid deposit insurance premiums to the FDIC to provide funds in case of bank failure. In 1993, U.S. banks began to pay the FDIC premiums based on their individual risk of failure. Before 1993, all banks that participated in the FDIC insurance program paid a flat amount, which means that banks with a low risk of failure as well as troubled banks paid the same amount per deposit. The change of policy led to greater responsibility on the part of many financial institutions.

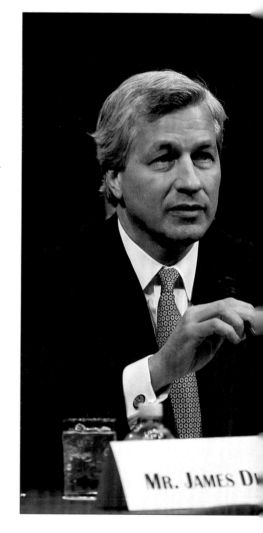

MR. JAMES D

The FDIC is also responsible for monitoring the recovery of failed banks. However, the FDIC's funds are not unlimited. The phenomenon of cascading bank failures could result in the depletion of the FDIC insurance fund that provides bank customers with a return of their funds after bank failure. In February 2009, the FDIC estimated that bank failures would cost the insurance fund around $65 billion through 2013, up from an earlier estimate of $40 billion. Additional banks failed in the intervening months. By July 2009, the FDIC was estimating its costs would be $70 billion through 2013.

James Dimon *(left)*, head of JPMorgan Chase, and Alan Schwartz *(right)*, head of Bear Stearns, testify to the U.S. Senate Banking, Housing, and Urban Affairs Committee on April 3, 2008.

Efforts to Resolve Bank Failures

While government agencies can provide depositor insurance to make up for the funds that failing banks have lost, other methods are also used to solve bank failures. Government regulators often arrange for a stronger bank to take over the assets of a failing bank. Sometimes, this is referred to as a "marriage" between financial institutions. The stronger bank is often able to manage the failing bank into a profitable status and is able to preserve the basic capital of depositors.

Referring to the U.S. mortgage crisis of 2008 and the rapid rise in bank failures, Joseph Mason, associate professor of finance at Drexel University's LeBow College of Business, tells *BusinessWeek* that "at this point in the crisis, you can't stop bank failures . . . you manage through failures and arrange marriages where another stronger bank takes on the assets and deposits. You move through the problem. You don't avoid the problem. It's too late to wait and hope that things get better."

IndyMac Bank was the first large financial institution to fail in the 2008 mortgage and financial crisis that eventually spread worldwide. It would not be the last large bank to fail. In September 2008, Washington Mutual, another California-based bank that specialized in mortgages and home equity loans, failed. Washington Mutual, also known as WaMu, was ten times the size of IndyMac. With $307 billion in assets at the time of its failure, WaMu was the largest bank failure in American history. The FDIC stepped in to assist in managing a transfer of Washington Mutual's customers and assets to another financial institution. After receiving bids from a number of other banks, JPMorgan Chase was selected as the bank that would be able to buy out Washington Mutual's assets and consolidate operations. Customers of Washington Mutual were transferred to new JPMorgan Chase accounts, and in many cases, Washington Mutual's offices remained open for business.

The U.S. Department of the Treasury also launched a program in which financial firms will buy as much as $40 billion worth of the mortgage-linked investments held by smaller banks that were at risk of failure. Other suggestions for resolving the banking crisis include maintaining the FDIC's "watch list" of banks with declining ratios of debt to capital and sending investigators to banks at the earliest sign of trouble.

Ten Great Questions
to Ask a Financial Adviser

1 How much money should I keep in my bank account?

2 How much money should I limit my deposits to, and why?

3 What should I do if I suspect that my bank could fail?

4 Should I try investing my money in alternative investments instead of a bank?

5 What are the advantages and disadvantages to saving money in a bank?

6 What are some techniques I can use to save money?

7 How can I save for college or a major purchase?

8 Should I get a credit card?

9 How can I make a financial plan?

10 How can I build a good credit history?

CHAPTER FIVE
Preventing Bank Failures

American, European, and Asian financial experts have studied bank failures throughout recent history and have determined several ways to prevent them. According to a 2004 study sponsored by the Bank for International Settlements, government can play an important role in limiting bank failures. The study concluded that government regulation and observation of banks can limit the number and cost of bank failures, but it isn't likely to prevent failures that are caused by large economic forces. Instead, regulation can prevent bank failures that result from fraud or misuse of funds.

Problem banks that are at risk of failure can be identified through frequent periodic bank examinations or visits by inspectors or regulators. In the United States, this is the job of the FDIC, and in Canada, banks are regulated by the Office of the Superintendent of Financial Institutions (OSFI). Deposit insurance, such as that provided by the FDIC, also helps to maintain stability through financial crises and bank

President Barack Obama greets bank executives at a business roundtable meeting on March 12, 2009, to discuss the financial crisis.

failures. The study found that the cost of deposit insurance can be high, however.

A 2000 analysis of the United States' savings and loan crisis calculated that the crisis cost U.S. taxpayers $123.8 billion, which represented more than 2 percent of the GDP in 1990.

The United States and other nations with mature economies, which include Western Europe, the United Kingdom, Australia, Canada, and Japan, all have government regulatory agencies that oversee banking. Each operates similarly to the FDIC. When economic crises strike, government regulatory agencies are authorized to increase fees to make sure that deposit insurance funds are able to cover the deposits of customers in failing banks. For example, in August 2009 the FDIC levied an emergency fee of $5.6 billion on banks, in addition to the annual charges that banks had already paid.

Regulators also use early warning systems that help identify potential bank failures as quickly as possible. One early warning system is called the "Texas ratio." During the 1980s, a series of bank failures in Texas encouraged financial expert Gerard Cassidy and others at RBC Capital Markets to develop a system for spotting potential financial trouble at banks. The Texas ratio system divides the bank's nonperforming loans (loans that cannot be paid back) by the company's reliable amounts of capital, plus money that the bank has set aside for loan losses. The resulting number measures credit problems as a percentage of the capital a bank has available to deal with them.

Some other countries with mature banking systems also operate with a lower risk, especially risk resulting from mortgage or real estate lending. Canada is one nation that has experienced lower rates of bank failure than nearly any other nation in the twentieth or twenty-first century.

Part of the history of bank failures can be understood by comparing banking systems in different countries. Laurence Booth, a professor of finance at the University of Toronto's Rotman School of Management, tells *Canadian Business* that differences between the United States' and Canada's banking systems existed as far back as the 1820s.

Americans distrusted their bankers from the beginning, Booth says, and "they were afraid of having a central bank." In 1816, Thomas Jefferson wrote that "banking establishments

Economists have studied bank failures for years. Past economic crises led to the formation of economic theories, including the ideas of Nobel Prize–winning economist Milton Friedman.

are more dangerous than standing armies, and that the principle of spending money to be paid by posterity, under the name of funding, is but swindling futurity on a large scale." Translated into modern terms, Jefferson did not want banks to lend too much money to customers. He thought that if the money was not able to be paid back in the future, other customers would lose the money that they had deposited in the bank. Thomas Jefferson's comment sounds like he was aware of the danger of bank failures.

Home Loans and Mortgages in Canada

American banks operate under U.S. laws and regulations meant to ensure fairness and nondiscrimination, which means that they must lend money to borrowers who may be less able than others to pay back loans. Canada lacks laws requiring banks to lend money to any borrower. Canada also lacks GSEs, like Fannie Mae and Freddie Mac, that offer affordable housing

Can Lessons Be Learned from Canada?

In August 2009, *Canadian Business* reported that the International Monetary Fund said that Canada's financial system appeared "to be in a position to weather financial turbulence." The World Economic Forum also called the Canadian system "one of the soundest in the world."

Canadian banks operate with much lower amounts of risk than American banks or most other banks in Europe and Asia. There are also fewer banks in Canada than in the United States. For example, thousands of American banks collapsed during the Great Depression of the 1930s. Economist Milton Friedman wrote in *A Monetary History of the United States* that during the 1930s, Canada's "10 banks with 3,000-odd branches throughout the country did not even experience any runs."

According to Canadian financial writer Matthew McClearn, only two Canadian banks have failed since 1923: the Canadian Commerce Bank and the Northland Bank of Canada. In 2009, there were about seventy banks in Canada, so some additional banks have been established since the 1930s.

Canadian bankers made different business choices from American, European, or Asian bankers during the housing bubble and mortgage crisis. In 2004 and 2005, Canadian banks purchased large amounts of mortgage-backed security funds.

However, due to questions about the safety and reliability of the mortgage-backed security funds, Canadian banks sold these funds after 2005.

guarantees for even those with a high risk of failure and that securitize high-risk loans by selling them to investors. Canadian banks hold a much larger share of direct home loans, and studies have shown that bank direct-held mortgages fail less often than securitized mortgages.

In the United States, the FHA's programs allow mortgages with a 3 percent down payment, and some mortgages were offered with no down payment. In Canada, if a down payment is less than 20 percent of the value of a home, a buyer must purchase mortgage insurance. Homeowners in the United States can abandon their loans if the balance on their

Government-sponsored housing entities, such as Freddie Mac and Fannie Mae, allowed high-risk borrowers to secure housing, which is said to have contributed to the housing crisis.

mortgage exceeds the value of the home. In this case, a U.S. bank's only option is to foreclose and sell the home for as much as it can get. According to August 2009 reports in *BusinessWeek* and on MSNBC, about one-third of American homeowners had mortgages for larger amounts than their homes were worth. In Canada, mortgage holders are held strictly responsible for their home loans. Even if they abandon the mortgage and allow the bank to foreclose on the residence, the bank may also launch claims against their other assets. This strict approach means that home buyers in Canada tend to pay off their loans at a high rate. About the same percentage of people are homeowners in the United States and in Canada. Canada's stricter loan policies have not prevented many people from purchasing homes.

A Look at the Future

Canada is smaller than the United States, but it is not 90 percent smaller. Canada has seventy banks throughout the entire nation, and banks may operate nationwide. Canada's five largest banks also operate as international financial institutions. In contrast, in 2009, the United States had 11,500 banks or lending institutions, which include savings and loans and credit unions. Until 1999, banks in the United States were prohibited from opening branches in other states. In the southern United States, banks were often limited to a single county, which led to many small banks and few larger ones in an area. With relaxed standards after 2000, the large U.S. banks began to open national networks, including Bank of America, Citibank, and JPMorgan Chase. JPMorgan Chase expanded its national presence by purchasing a failed bank, Washington Mutual. However, even the largest U.S. bank did not have nationwide coverage. As of 2009, no bank in the United States operates branches in all fifty states.

This contributes to a U.S. banking system that is cumbersome and fragmented, especially for businesses that operate nationwide. Internationally, a number of countries successfully instituted electronic banking for businesses and individuals, which increased efficiency and reduced costs. In the United States, the use of electronic banking rose rapidly for individual customers in 2008 and 2009. According to Professor Dubos Masson of the Kelley School of Business at Indiana University, Bloomington, business transactions in the United States were still conducted primarily by mail and paper checks.

Checks written by payers are cleared for payment by the Federal Reserve Bank, a process that usually takes two to three days. Masson says that businesses continued to require paper bills to be sent in the mail, and they also wanted to respond by paying bills with a paper check that was mailed. In addition, U.S. businesses that operate in multiple states, including nationwide, often require banking relationships with dozens, and even hundreds, of local banks. Reducing the fragmentation and increasing efficiency by adopting electronic transfers for businesses as well as individual customers could improve bank productivity and reduce the potential for future bank failures. Reducing paper check use can also be good for the environment.

Before the mortgage crisis and bank failures of 2008, many financial experts thought that extreme financial risk was a thing

Banking behemoths, such as Citigroup, will have to change their business models in the future in order to avoid future financial meltdowns.

of the past. The regulations and deposit insurance that were instituted by the United States and many other countries after the Great Depression of the 1930s seemed to be protection against the kind of financial panic and bank runs that occurred during those years. Financial experts also relied upon computers and electronic tracking systems to identify and alert regulators to potential bank failures. The experts did not account for the complexity of mortgage-backed securities which seemed at first like a positive way to reduce financial risk when they were first used by banks. The losses related to mortgage-backed securities turned out to be much greater than any bank or expert could have imagined.

The future will hold more caution for banks, bank customers, and regulatory agencies in all countries with large banking systems. A term used by financial experts is moral hazard, which refers to the willingness for banks, insurance companies, and other financial institutions to take excessive risks knowing that the government will bail them out if they fail. For banks to succeed in the future, the moral hazard factor should play a smaller role. While governments play an important role in regulating banks, preventing failures, and helping to repay customer deposits in the case of failure, nearly everyone can agree that rather than trying to fix a failing bank, it is better for the bank to remain stable and successful for the well-being of customers and the public alike.

GLOSSARY

adjustable mortgage A loan for home purchase with an interest rate that will adjust as economic conditions change. Most adjustable mortgages start with very low interest rates, which create low monthly payments, and adjust to higher rates, which create higher payments.

assets The combination of cash, investments, and property that a corporation or individual has available. A liquid asset is one that can be quickly converted to cash, and fixed assets are property, equipment, or supplies.

capital The amount of money and assets owned by a business, bank, or individual.

credit The amount of money a lender is willing to lend and a borrower is able to borrow.

credit crunch A loss of available credit for loans, including lending between banks for business loans, mortgages, and personal loans.

debt The sum of money that an individual, company, or bank owes as the result of a mortgage, loan, or other extension of credit.

deflation A reduction in the cost of goods and services, often caused by a reduction in the supply of money or credit.

embezzlement The act of taking money that has been placed in one person's trust or control, but belongs to another person. For instance, someone who works in a bank may secretly steal money that he or she has been entrusted to look after.

equity The amount or percentage of the value of a mortgaged property that a person (or bank) owns.

FDIC The Federal Deposit Insurance Corporation is a U.S. government agency established to insure the bank deposits of Americans after the bank failures that occurred during the Great Depression in the 1930s.

foreclosure The legal procedure where a lender takes the right to have a property away from the person who agreed to pay for it in installments over time (mortgage).

FSLIC The Federal Savings and Loan Insurance Company is a similar organization to the FDIC that insured deposits at savings and loans between 1934 and 1989. The FSLIC became bankrupt and its duties were assumed by the FDIC in 1989.

GSEs Government-sponsored enterprises (GSEs) are private businesses established by the government. Mortgage lenders Fannie Mae and Freddie Mac are both GSEs.

inflation A steady rise in the cost of products and services.

liquidity The amount of money a bank or individual has on hand to pay immediate obligations.

mortgage The transfer of interest in a property, such as land and buildings, as security for a debt (an agreement to pay money). The original word is based on a French word meaning "dead pledge." A dead pledge means that the agreement stops when the debtor dies or the property is taken by foreclosure.

obligations In banking and finance, obligations represent agreements to pay money to creditors or investors.

prime rate The basic short-term interest rate in the banking system of the United States. All financial institutions use the prime rate as a basis for providing loans and mortgages to customers.

subprime mortgage A mortgage with significantly higher risk than a traditional or prime mortgage. The loan-to-equity ratio (the amount of the loan versus the value of the property being purchased) may be negative, and borrowers may have many high-risk factors, such as low-income or previously poor credit.

FOR MORE INFORMATION

Bank of Canada
Currency Museum
245 Sparks Street
Ottawa, ON K1A 0G9
Canada
(613) 782-8914
Web site: http://www.bankofcanada.ca/currencymuseum
The Bank of Canada's Currency Museum was opened in 1980.
   It is home to the National Currency Collection, the largest
   collection of Canadian bank notes, coins, and tokens in the
   world. The museum is located within the first Bank of
   Canada building (built in 1934) in Ottawa.

Department of Finance Canada
Consultations and Communications Branch
19th Floor, East Tower
140 O'Connor Street
Ottawa, ON K1A 0G5
Canada
Web site: http://www.fin.gc.ca
This department of Canadian government is responsible for
   administering regulations and monitoring and reporting on
   Canada's banking system.

Federal Deposit Insurance Corporation (FDIC)
External Affairs
550 17th Street NW
Washington, DC 20429
(877) 275-3342
Web site: http://www.fdic.gov
An independent agency of the federal government, the
   FDIC was created in 1933 in response to the thousands
   of bank failures that occurred in the 1920s and early 1930s.
   Since the start of FDIC insurance on January 1, 1934, no
   depositor has lost a single cent of insured funds as a result
   of a failure.

Federal Reserve Bank of San Francisco
Consumer Affairs Office
San Francisco Office
101 Market Street, MS 215
San Francisco, CA 94105
(415) 974-2765
Web site: http://www.frbsf.org
In addition to their activity as regional bank coordinators and
clearinghouses, all twelve Federal Reserve Banks provide
information for consumers, students, and educators as well as
bank industry employees and organizations. They conduct
training sessions for consumers, businesses, and finance pro-
fessionals in their regions.

National Foundation for Credit Counseling
801 Roeder Road, Suite 900
Silver Spring, MD 20910

(800) 388-2227
Web site: http://www.nfcc.org
The NFCC is the largest and longest-serving national
nonprofit credit counseling network in the United
States, with more than 100 member agencies and
nearly 850 offices in communities throughout the
country. Each year, NFCC members assist more than
3.2 million consumers, helping many to take control of
their finances.

Office of the Comptroller of the Currency (OCC)
Communications Division
One Independence Square
Washington, DC 20219
(202) 874-4700
Web site: http://www.occ.treas.gov
The Office of the Comptroller of the Currency (OCC)
charters, regulates, and supervises all national banks. It
also supervises the federal branches and agencies of foreign
banks. Headquartered in Washington, D.C., the OCC has
four district offices plus an office in London to supervise
the international activities of national banks.

Office of the Superintendent of Bankruptcy Canada
Heritage Place
155 Queen Street, 4th Floor
Ottawa, ON K1A 0H5
Canada
(613) 941-1000
Web site: http://www.ic.gc.ca

Canada's Office of the Superintendent of Bankruptcy offers
    many services to Canadian consumers, including advice on
    finances, credit counseling, debt management programs,
    and many alternatives to bankruptcy.

U.S. Financial Literacy and Education Commission
c/o the Federal Citizen Information Center
Pueblo, CO 81009
(888) MY-MONEY [696-6639]
Web site: http://www.mymoney.gov
This U.S. government–sponsored commission is responsible
    for providing financial education, training, and guidance
    to all citizens, including teens. The Web site is part of the
    Federal Citizen Information Center's group of Web sites
    for consumer and citizen information.

Web Sites

Due to the changing nature of Internet links, Rosen
Publishing has developed an online list of Web sites related to
the subject of this book. This site is updated regularly. Please
use this link to access the list:

http://www.rosenlinks.com/rwe/bank

FOR FURTHER READING

Belliner, Karen, editor. *Cash and Credit Information for Teens.* Detroit, MI: Omnigraphics, 2009.

Berntzen, Katherine. *In Pursuit of My Success for Teens: Developing a College, Career, and Money Plan for Life.* Chicago, IL: Katherine Berntzen, 2009.

Blatt, Jessica. *The Teen Girl's Gotta Have It Guide to Money.* New York, NY: Watson-Guptill, 2007.

Espejo, Roman. *Teens and Credit.* Farmington Hills, MI: Greenhaven, 2009.

Foster, Chad. *Financial Literacy for Teens.* Conyers, GA: Rising Books, 2004.

Harman, Hollis Page. *Money Sense for Kids.* Hauppage, NY: Barrons, 2005.

Kiyosaki, Robert T. *Rich Dad, Poor Dad for Teens: The Secrets About Money That You Don't Learn in School!* Philadelphia, PA: Running Press, 2009.

Silver, Don. *High School Money Book.* Los Angeles, CA: Adams-Hall, 2006.

Spinks-Burleson, Kimberly. *Prepare to be a Teen Millionaire.* Deerfield Beach, FL: HCI Books, 2008.

Women's Foundation of California. *It's a Money Thing! A Girl's Guide to Managing Money.* San Francisco, CA: Chronicle Books, 2008.

BIBLIOGRAPHY

Barr, Alastair. "Bank Failures to Surge as Credit Crunch Slows Economy." May 23, 2008. Retrieved June 26, 2009. (http://www.marketwatch.com/story/bank-failures-surge-credit-crunch).

Basel Committee on Banking Supervision. "Working Paper #13: Bank Failures in Mature Economies." Bank for International Settlements, April 2004.

Bernanke, Ben. *Essays on the Great Depression*. Princeton, NJ: Princeton University Press, 2000.

Boston Globe. "More Scrutiny for New Banks: FDIC Increases Its Oversight." August 29, 2009, p. B7.

Byrnes, Nanette. "How Customers Catch Bank Run Fever." *BusinessWeek*, June 1, 2009.

Chu, Kathy. "How Bank Failures Happen and What They Mean." *USA Today*, July 18, 2008. Retrieved June 20, 2009 (http://www.usatoday.com/money/industries/banking/2008-07-13-how-do-bank-failures-happen_N.htm).

Cohen, Edward E. *Athenian Economy and Society: A Banking Perspective*. Princeton, NJ: Princeton University Press, 1992.

Dixon Murray, Teresa. "How Banks Fail and What It Means to You." Cleveland.com, September 26, 2008. Retrieved June 20, 2009 (http://blog.cleveland.com/business/2008/09/how_banks_fail_and_what_it_mea.html).

Economist. "Finance and Economics: Sweaty Days; Banks in the Deep South." August 29, 2009, Vol. 392, No. 8646, p. 65.

Federal Deposit Insurance Corporation. "Failed Bank List." June 19, 2009. Retrieved June 20, 2009 (http://www.fdic.gov/bank/individual/failed/banklist.html).

Friedman, Milton, and Anna Jacobson Schwartz. *A Monetary History of the United States, 1867–1960.* 5th ed. Princeton, NJ: Princeton University Press, 1971.

Gordon, Marcy. "Bank Failures Rise to 55 FDIC Insured Banks This Year." Retrieved July 10, 2009. (http://www.wcnc.com/news/consumer/68729197.html).

Gordon, Marcy. "FDIC Expects Bank Failures to Cost More, Hikes Fees." February 27, 2009. Retrieved June 26, 2009 (http://www.usatoday.com/money/industries/banking/2009-02-27-fdic-fees_N.htm).

Gray, Christopher. "Streetscapes: The Bank of the United States in the Bronx; The First Domino in the Depression." *New York Times*, August 18, 1991. Retrieved June 26, 2009 (http://www.nytimes.com/1991/08/18/realestate/streetscapes-bank-united-states-bronx-first-domino-depression.html).

Gup, Benton E. *Bank Failures in the Major Trading Companies of the World: Causes and Remedies.* Westport, CT: Greenwood Book, 1998.

Keeler, Dan. "World's 50 Safest Banks." *Global Finance*, April 1, 2009.

Kravis, Marie-Josée. "Regulation Didn't Save Canadian Banks." *Wall Street Journal*, May 7, 2009. Retrieved June 20, 2009 (http://online.wsj.com/article/SB124165325829393691.html).

Kristof, Kathy M. "IndyMac Bank Seized by Federal Regulators." *Los Angeles Times*, July 12, 2008. Retrieved June 20, 2009 (http://articles.latimes.com/2008/jul/12/business/fi-indymac12).

Lowry, Kim E., ed. "A Year in Bank Supervision." *Supervisory Insights*, Summer 2009. Retrieved June 20, 2009 (http://www.fdic.gov/regulations/examinations/supervisory/insights/sisum09/si_sum09.pdf).

Masson, Dubos J. "Commercial Banking in the U.S. Versus Canada." *Graziadio Business Report*, Vol. 10, Issue 7, 2007 (http://gbr.pepperdine.edu/074/bank.html).

McClearn, Matthew. "Last Banks Standing." *Canadian Business*, Summer 2009, Volume 82, Issue 8/9.

100777.com. "What Is a Trillion Dollars?" September 23, 2003. Retrieved June 20, 2009 (http://100777.com/node/455).

Schoen, John W. "Seven Lessons from the Financial Meltdown." *MSNBC Business: Economy in Turmoil*. Retrieved September 11, 2009. (http://www.msnbc.msn.com/id/32544407/ns/business-economy_in_turmoil/).

Terhune, Chad, and Robert Berner. "Florida Sub-Prime Mortgages." *BusinessWeek*, December 1, 2008, Issue 4110.

Walter, John R. "Depression-Era Bank Failures: The Great Contagion or the Great Shakeout?" *Economic Quarterly*, Winter 2005, Vol. 91 Issue 1.

Zakaria, Fareed. "Worthwhile Canadian Initiative." *Newsweek*, February 7, 2009. Retrieved June 20, 2009 (http://www.newsweek.com/id/183670).

INDEX

About the Author

Amy Sterling Casil is an award-nominated writer. She has published twenty books, including several written for the Rosen Publishing Group. She has a master's degree in literature and creative writing from Chapman University in Orange, California, and has taught composition and literature in diverse southern California classrooms for ten years. Since 2005, she has also served as the vice president for development with Beyond Shelter, a nationally recognized nonprofit organization. Casil has more than ten years of executive-level experience in nonprofit accounting and federal audit standards.

Photo Credits

Cover (top) © www.istockphoto.com/Lilli Day; cover (bottom), p. 1 Kate Gillon/Getty Images; pp. 6, 65 © Mario Tama/ Getty Images; pp. 8–9 © Gabriel Bouys/Getty Images; pp. 11, 51 © Alex Wong/Getty Images; pp. 14–15 © Getty Images; pp. 18–19, 33 © www.istockphoto.com; pp. 20–21 © Joe Raedle/Getty Images; pp. 26–27 © Robert Giroux/Getty Images; pp. 28–29 © Spencer Platt/Getty Images; pp. 34–35 © FDIC; pp. 38–39 © Chris Kleponis/AFP/Getty Images; pp. 40–41 © www.istockphoto.com/Dan Eckert; p. 45 © Ethan Miller/Getty Images; p. 47 © Maxim Shipenkov/AFP/ Getty Images; pp. 52–53 © Mark Wilson/Getty Images; p. 58 © Mandel Ngan/Getty Images; p. 60 © Staff/AFP/Getty Images; p. 62 © Paul J. Richards/AFP/Getty Images.

Designer: Sam Zavieh; Editor: Nicholas Croce;
Photo Researcher: Marty Levick